Name ______________________

AF732460

1 What Is a Sentence?

The children open their eyes.

The morning begins.

Draw lines to match the groups of words to make sentences. Then write the sentences.

1. The sun	barks.
2. The dog	rises.
3. Dad	hurry.
4. We	calls.
5. Breakfast	tastes good.

1. ______________________

2. ______________________

3. ______________________

4. ______________________

5. ______________________

Name ________________________

1 What Is a Sentence? (continued from page 1)

Challenge

Draw lines to match the groups of words to make sentences. Then write the poem.

1.	I	are baking.
2.	The day	grins.
3.	Rolls	am waking.
4.	Everyone	begins.

____

____

____

____

Writing Application: A Sentence

NARRATING

Write a sentence about what you like to eat for breakfast.

____

Table of Contents

Name ______________________

2 Naming Part

The children have a parade.

Their parade goes down the sidewalk.

A baby	Bess	Balloons	Leo	The dog

Look at the picture. Write a naming part from the Word Box to begin each sentence about the picture.

1. ______________________ holds a flag.

2. ______________________ plays the horn.

3. ______________________ fly behind Leo.

4. ______________________ hits the drum.

5. ______________________ walks last.

Name ______________________

2 Naming Part (continued from page 3)

Challenge

Make your own silly animal parade. Write a naming part to begin each sentence. Use animal names. Then draw your silly animal parade on another sheet of paper.

Example _____ leads the parade.

A monkey leads the parade.

1. ______________________ rings a bell.
2. ______________________ rides a bike.
3. ______________________ waves.

Writing Application: A Sentence

DESCRIBING

Write a sentence that describes a parade you might have with your friends.

____

Grade 2: Unit 1 The Sentence *(Use with pupil book pages 29–30.)*
Skill: Students will write the subjects of sentences and one original sentence.

Grammar

Name ______________________________

3 Action Part

> You **see many animals in the city.**
>
> Animals **live all around.**

Look at the picture. Write an action part from the Word Box to finish each sentence.

fly in the air	bark at the cats	sit in a tree
run along wires	hop in the grass	

1. Squirrels ______________________________.

2. Birds ______________________________.

3. Dogs ______________________________.

4. Rabbits ______________________________.

5. Cats ______________________________.

Name ______________________________

3 Action Part (continued from page 5)

Challenge

Find the action part from the Word Box that fits each sentence. Then write each action part in the correct place in the puzzle.

sing	eat nuts	make tunnels
meow	wag tails	carry riders

ACROSS

2. Ants ___?___.
4. Birds ___?___.
5. Dogs ___?___.
6. Cats ___?___.

DOWN

1. Horses ___?___.
3. Squirrels ___?___.

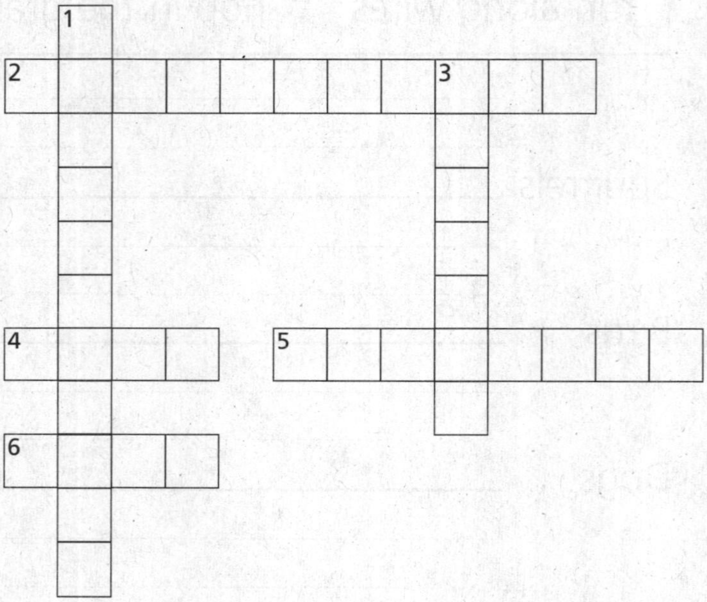

Writing Application: A Sentence

INFORMING

Write a sentence about an animal you might see in the city.

____

____

Grade 2: Unit 1 The Sentence *(Use with pupil book pages 31–32.)*
Skill: Students will write the predicates of sentences and a new sentence.

Name ______________________

4 Is It a Sentence?

naming part | action part

Lightning + flashed last night.

Lightning flashed last night.

Draw a line under the sentence in each pair. Then write the sentences.

1. Now the sky is clear.
Is clear today.

2. I sit on the top step.
The front steps.

3. My best friend Cora.
Cora sits below me.

4. Clapping and singing.
Cora and I sing songs.

Name ______________________________

4 Is It a Sentence? (continued from page 7)

Challenge

Bobby Short takes shortcuts. He took too many shortcuts when he wrote this story. Read his story. Then write the story, using sentences. Write the story on another sheet of paper.

Once upon a time a boy
and his mother
poor
no food or money
big storm
Thunder and lightning
crashed
hidden under the tree
a treasure chest
lots of gold and silver
jewels shining
in the tree
helped their friends
lived happily ever after

Writing Application: A Sentence

DESCRIBING

Write a sentence about your street.

____

____

Grade 2: Unit 1 The Sentence *(Use with pupil book pages 33–34.)*
Skill: Students will rewrite a story using sentences. They will write an original sentence.

Name ______________________________

Writing Complete Sentences

Complete Sentence

naming part	**action part**
Puppies	play all day.

Completing Sentences 1–5. Add a naming part to each underlined group of words. Write the new paragraph.

Our new puppy is brown. Teaches the puppy to sit. Have fun playing with it. He likes to bark. Chews on a little toy. Gave him a ball. Sleeps in my bed.

Name ______________________________

Writing Complete Sentences

Complete Sentence

naming part	action part
The circus	starts at 7 o'clock.

Completing Sentences Add an action part to each underlined group of words. Write the new sentences.

The tall clown danced in the ring. The circus horses. Then a man. He rode the horses all around. A big elephant. The elephant. The circus.

1. ______________________________

2. ______________________________

3. ______________________________

4. ______________________________

5. ______________________________

Grade 2: Unit 1 The Sentence *(Use with pupil book page 36.)*
Skill: Students will write complete sentences.

Name ______________________

5 Telling Sentences

Grandfather has a special pet. **I**t lives in a large cage.

A Write these telling sentences correctly.

1. grandfather has a parrot.

____

2. its name is Roberto.

____

3. It eats seeds and fruit

____

B **4–6.** Proofread this part of an article. Find five mistakes with capital letters and end marks. Correct each mistake.

Example ~~josh~~ Josh read an article about parrots.

Proofreading

You can teach a parrot words Many parrots love to talk. all parrots have huge bills they use their bills for cracking seeds

Name ______________________

5 Telling Sentences (continued from page 11)

Challenge

Roberto wants to talk to you, but his sentences are mixed up. Write the words in each sentence in the correct order. Use capital letters and periods correctly.

1. ______________________

2. ______________________

3. ______________________

4. ______________________

Writing Application: A Sentence

INFORMING

Write a sentence that tells about a noisy pet.

____

Grade 2: Unit 1 The Sentence *(Use with pupil book pages 37–38.)*
Skill: Students will write statements, using capital letters and periods.

Name ______________________________

6 Questions

What is a rainbow**? W**hich colors are in a rainbow**?**

A Write the questions correctly.

1. what makes a rainbow?

____

2. is the rain in front of you?

____

3. is the sun behind you

____

B **4–8.** Proofread these instructions. Find two incorrect small letters and add three missing question marks. Correct each mistake.

Example ~~do~~ Do you like rainbows?

Proofreading

would you like to see a rainbow Where should you be is the sun behind you? Is the rain in front

You may see a rainbow.

Name ______________________

6 Questions (continued from page 13)

Challenge

Read the following answers to riddles about colors. Write a question above each riddle answer.

Example What colors make green?
Blue and yellow make green.

1. ______________________
Red and yellow make orange.

2. ______________________
Rose is a color and a flower.

3. ______________________
Orange is a color and something to eat.

Writing Application: A Question

DESCRIBING

Write a question about a rainbow.

____

____

____

Grade 2: Unit 1 The Sentence *(Use with pupil book pages 39–40.)*
Skill: Students will write questions, using capital letters and question marks.

Name ______________________________

7 Which Kind of Sentence?

Telling Sentence: We have a pond in our yard**.**

Question: Do you swim in your pond**?**

A Write each telling sentence or question correctly.

1. what lives in this pond

____

2. turtles and fish live here

____

3. plants grow on the bottom

____

B **4–8.** Proofread this part of a post card. Find two sentences that need capital letters and three sentences that need end marks. Correct each mistake.

Example ~~is~~ Is there a pond near your home?

Proofreading

I have a pond near my house What do we see

there there are frogs and fish. there is a turtle

Name ________________________________

7 Which Kind of Sentence? (continued from page 15)

Challenge

A spider has made a word web. Read the words in the web. Write two telling sentences and two questions, using words that are joined together. Write your sentences on another sheet of paper. Here is an idea for one sentence.

Example I like turtles.

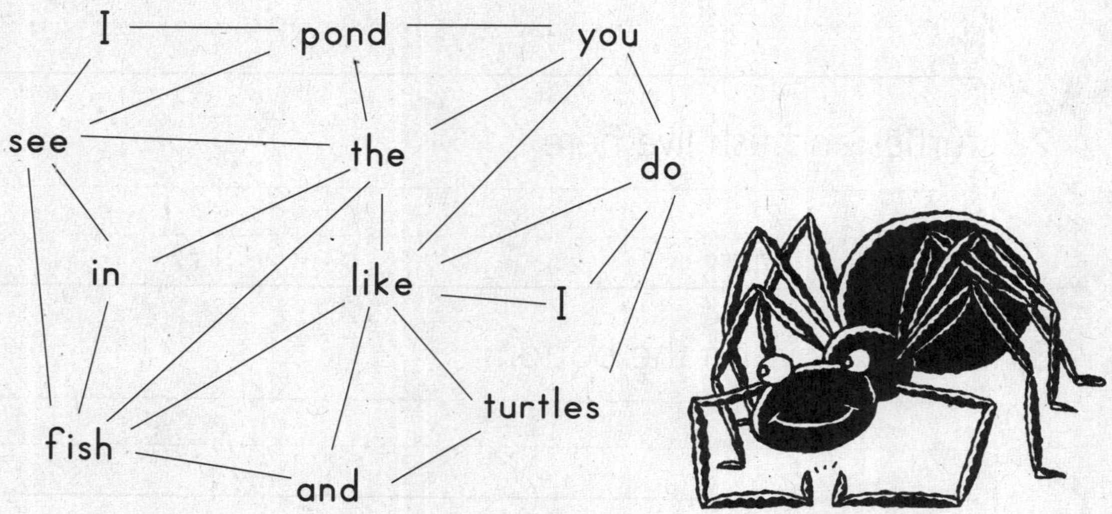

Writing Application: Sentences

INFORMING

Write a telling sentence about a raccoon's visit to the pond.

____

Write a question about the pond in the winter.

____

Grade 2: Unit 1 The Sentence *(Use with pupil book pages 41–42.)*
Skill: Students will write statements and questions correctly.

Name ____________________

8 Commands

Take this ball.

Follow me.

Write these commands correctly.

1. Watch the ball

2. Hit the ball?

3. run to first base

4. stop there?

5. wait for the next hitter.

6. run to second base.

Name ____________________

8 Commands (continued from page 17)

Challenge

Look at the treasure map. Read the words around the sides. Then write four commands using the words. You can use each word as many times as you like. Write your commands on another sheet of paper. Here is an idea for one sentence.

Example Find the tree.

Writing Application: Commands

EXPLAINING

Write a command telling how to find a toy in your home.

Grade 2: Unit 1 The Sentence *(Use with pupil book pages 43–44.)*
Skill: Students will write commands correctly.

Name ______________________________

9 Exclamations

A big storm is coming tonight!

The waves will be 12 feet high!

A Draw a line under each correct exclamation.

1. The wind is blowing really hard.
The wind is blowing really hard!

2. Watch out for falling trees!
Watch out for falling trees.

B **3–6.** Proofread this part of a weather report. Find two words that need capital letters. Add a missing end mark and change another one.

Example ~~don't~~ Don't leave the house tonight !

Proofreading

There is a storm coming tonight. The storm will start around 8 o'clock. watch out The rain will be very hard. don't go onto the beach?

Name ____________________

9 Exclamations (continued from page 19)

Challenge

Look at the picture. Then write four exclamations that tell about the picture.

1. ____________________

2. ____________________

3. ____________________

4. ____________________

Writing Application: An Exclamation

EXPRESSING

Write your own exclamation about a big storm.

____

Grade 2: Unit 1 The Sentence *(Use with pupil book pages 45–46.)*
Skill: Students will write exclamations correctly.

Name ______________________________

Telling Enough Details

Not enough: I had fun.

Enough: I had fun in the play.

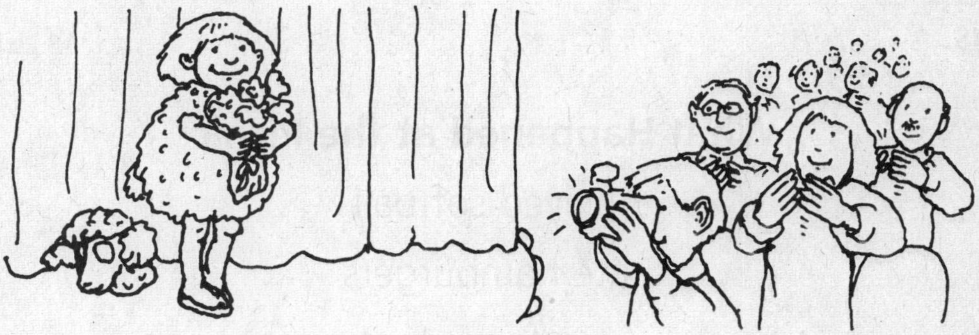

Look at this picture. Complete the Five W's Chart below for the story idea.

Five W's Chart
What happened?
Who was there?
Why did it happen?
When did it happen?
Where did it happen?

Name ______________________________

Keeping to the Topic

> The picnic was fun. We played lots of games. ~~Dad is tall~~. The hot dogs were tasty.

Read this list. Cross out things that do not belong. Write a sentence that tells why you chose these things.

What Happened at the Picnic

played softball

ate hamburgers

made my bed

sat in the grass

washed the windows

smelled the flowers

Grade 2: Unit 2 Personal Narrative *(Use with pupil book page 72.)*
Skill: Students will identify items that do not keep to a topic.

Name ____________________

Revising a Personal Narrative

Have I	**yes**
• written an interesting beginning?	☐
• added enough details?	☐
• kept to the topic?	☐
• ended in an interesting way?	☐

Revise this narrative to make it better. Check off each box to be sure. You can write your changes in the spaces above each line, on the sides, and below the paragraph.

I had an adventure. Where I live, it rains a lot. One year, it rained so much that it flooded. The rivers rose higher than the road. We live on a hill and we got trapped. The first day, he rowed the canoe to the store to get food. I think that store is pretty good. Then a helicopter came to rescue us. We stayed at my cousins' house for a week.

Name ______________________

Revising Strategies: Sentence Fluency

I went to visit Aunt Carole.
~~I went to see~~ I visited my four cousins.

Revise one sentence in each pair, so the sentences have different beginnings.

1. Orin wanted to work on his tree house. Orin wanted to buy nails at the hardware store.

2. I was helping Orin all day. I was using a hammer and a saw.

3. Orin had finished his plans. Orin had some friends help.

Grade 2: Unit 2 Personal Narrative *(Use with pupil book page 78.)*
Skill: Students will revise words in sentences to vary them.

Name ____________________

1 Nouns

A **writer** can write about many things.

Write the noun that names a person in each sentence.

1. My grandmother writes stories. ____________

2. A sailor might cross a stormy sea. ____________

3. A boy might win a contest. ____________

4. A king might rule a strange land. ____________

5. A girl could meet a friendly lion. ____________

6. My brother loves the stories. ____________

7. My friend reads the stories. ____________

8. My father tells good stories too. ____________

Grammar Name ______________________

1 Nouns (continued from page 25)

Challenge

Some nouns are missing from Emma's letter. Write a noun that names a person on each line. Use the nouns from the Word Box or your own words.

brother	aunt	friend	doctor	painter
sister	dentist	sailor	teacher	grandfather

Dear Marcos,

Please come to my costume party. My little ______________ is dressing up as a ______________. My ______________ is going to be a ______________. I will be a ______________. I'll see you there.

Your ______________,

Emma

Writing Application: Sentences

NARRATING

Write four sentences that tell about exciting story ideas. Use a noun that names a person in each sentence.

Grade 2: Unit 3 Nouns and Pronouns *(Use with pupil book pages 93–94.)*
Skill: Students will write nouns that name people. They will write original sentences using nouns.

Grammar

Name ______________________

2 More Nouns

person	thing	place

Cleo lives in a **building** near the **park**.

A Write the nouns that name places or things.

1. We live in the city. ______________________

2. Our apartment is big. ______________________

3. My room is sunny. ______________________

4. I love the big window. ______________________

B Write the noun in each row.

5. add cat sad ______________________

6. then tall cave ______________________

7. fork far first ______________________

8. open late home ______________________

Name ____________________

2 More Nouns (continued from page 27)

Challenge

Finish this list for Lin. Look at the words in the Word Box. Write the names of the three places under PLACES TO GO. Then write the things that Lin needs to get under the name of the correct place.

bread	leaves	market	library
bookmark	rocks	acorns	milk
park	cheese	books	tapes

PLACES TO GO

______ ______ ______

THINGS TO GET

______ ______ ______

______ ______ ______

______ ______ ______

______ ______ ______

Writing Application: A Description

DESCRIBING

Write a description of a strange land. What is it like? What things are in it?

Grade 2: Unit 3 Nouns and Pronouns *(Use with pupil book pages 95–96.)*
Skill: Students will identify and write nouns that name places or things. They will write a description of a place.

Name ______________________

3 One and More Than One

one bird	three **birds**
a gate	many **gates**

In each sentence, two nouns have lines drawn under them. Write the noun that names more than one.

1. My friends and I went to the zoo. ______________
2. The animals ran to the fence. ______________
3. A tiger played with its cubs. ______________
4. We saw the bears after lunch. ______________
5. They played games in their cave. ______________
6. A worker fed the elephants. ______________
7. We saw ducks in a pond. ______________
8. Their legs paddled in the water. ______________

Name ______________________________

3 One and More Than One (continued from page 29)

Challenge

Read Tom's letter. Write nouns that name more than one in the blanks. Use the nouns that name one in the Word Box to help you.

lion	elephant	friend	cub	bird	bear	tree

Dear Edward,

My ______________ and I went to the zoo. We saw a tiger playing with some ______________. We saw the ______________. One was very funny. We saw all kinds of ______________. I liked the ______________ best of all.

Your friend,

Tom

Writing Application: A Story

NARRATING

Write a story about something your class did. Use nouns that name more than one in your story.

Grade 2: Unit 3 Nouns and Pronouns *(Use with pupil book pages 97–98.)*
Skill: Students will form plural nouns by adding *s*. They will write an original story using plural nouns.

Name ______________________________

Combining Sentences: Naming Parts

Two sentences:	Nina looked at the snow. Luc looked at the snow.
One sentence:	**Nina** and **Luc** looked at the snow.

Joining Naming Parts 1-4. Look at the underlined sentence pairs. Join the naming parts in each pair. Write the new paragraph.

The snow fell. The sleet fell. Nina wanted to go out to play. Luc wanted to go out to play. Mom said no. Dad said no. Nina asked again. Luc asked again. The weather was fine now!

Name ______________________________

Combining Sentences: Naming Parts

Two sentences:	The squirrel ate nuts. The bird ate nuts.
One sentence:	**The squirrel** and **the bird** ate nuts.

Joining Naming Parts Read each underlined sentence pair. Join the naming parts. Write the new sentences.

Different animals eat different kinds of foods. Nuts are good for birds. Seeds are good for birds. Mice like acorns. Squirrels like acorns. Turtles eat bugs. Frogs eat bugs. Horses eat hay. Goats eat hay. I like milk and cereal.

1. ______________________________

2. ______________________________

3. ______________________________

4. ______________________________

Grade 2: Unit 3 Nouns and Pronouns *(Use with pupil book pages 99–100.)*
Skill: Students will combine sentences and write new sentences.

Grammar

Name ______________________

4 Nouns with es

a dress	**two dresses**	a bunch	**some bunches**
one fox	**many foxes**	one glass	**six glasses**

A Write the sentences. Make the underlined noun name more than one.

1. Ana's house has two porch.

____

2. Bush grow by the back porch.

____

3. I give Ana's mother two kiss.

____

B **4–5.** Proofread this part of a story. Find two nouns that should name more than one. Correct each mistake.

Example Ana has three ~~bunch~~ bunches of flowers.

Proofreading

The girls had two box. Each box had a branch. Ana planted the two branch.

Name ______________________

4 Nouns with es (continued from page 33)

Challenge

Write each noun to name more than one. Then find the nouns that name more than one in the puzzle. Circle them.

Example patch patches

1. kiss ______________

2. ranch ______________

3. bush ______________

4. class ______________

5. fox ______________

R	A	N	C	H	E	S
P	A	T	C	H	E	S
F	K	I	L	O	N	K
O	P	T	A	Q	B	I
X	U	R	S	C	U	S
E	B	U	S	H	E	S
S	H	Z	E	L	N	E
X	O	T	S	G	T	S

Writing Application: Sentences

INFORMING

Write sentences about the buses that come at the end of the school day.

Grade 2: Unit 3 Nouns and Pronouns *(Use with pupil book pages 101–102.)*
Skill: Students will form plural nouns by adding es and write original sentences.

Name ______________________________

5 Nouns That Change Spelling

one child	many **children**
a man	three **men**
one woman	four **women**

Write the correct noun in each sentence. Read the sentences to be sure that they make sense.

1. Two ________________ own Kim's building.
(woman, women)

2. Kim knows most of the ________________ there.
(child, children)

3. One ________________ goes to Kim's school.
(child, children)

4. A ________________ brings in the mail each day.
(woman, women)

5. Three ________________ fix Kim's building.
(man, men)

6. One ________________ worked on the pipes last week.
(man, men)

Name ______________________

5 Nouns That Change Spelling (continued from page 35)

Challenge

Use the secret code to find more nouns that change their spelling to name more than one. Write the letter for each number in the space above the number.

SECRET CODE

a 1	**c** 2	**d** 3	**e** 4	**f** 5	**g** 6	**h** 7	**i** 8	**l** 9
m 10	**n** 11	**o** 12	**p** 13	**r** 14	**s** 15	**t** 16	**u** 17	**w** 18

1. Two ______________ live on a farm.
   (10–8–2–4)

2. Three ______________ live on the farm too.
   (6–4–4–15–4)

3. Some ______________ take care of the animals.
   (13–4–12–13–9–4)

Writing Application: A Story

NARRATING

Write a story about people who live on a small island. Use the nouns men, women, and children.

Grade 2: Unit 3 Nouns and Pronouns *(Use with pupil book pages 103–104.)*
Skill: Students will write nouns that change their spelling in plural form. They will write an original story.

Name ____________________

6 Special Nouns

Nouns		Special Nouns	
man	street	**D**on	**P**ine **S**treet
town	pet	**S**pringville	**I**nky

A Write the special nouns correctly.

1. We live in seatown. ____________

2. We both live on fly road. ____________

3. He has a dragonfly named puff. ____________

4. I have a spider named legsly. ____________

B **5–8.** Proofread this part of an invitation. Find four special nouns that should be changed. Correct each mistake.

Example Come to a party for ~~janis~~ Janis!

Proofreading

Please join us for a party! It is julio's birthday.

Saturday, march 18 at 3 o'clock

115 beaver Street, oakmont

Name ____________________

6 Special Nouns (continued from page 37)

Challenge

Finish these sentences with your own special nouns.

1. My full name is ____________________.
2. If I could change my name, I would change it to ____________________.
3. I live on ____________________.
4. I live in ____________________.
5. If I could live anywhere, I would live in ____________________.
6. If I had a pet grasshopper, I would name it ____________________.

Writing Application: A Story

NARRATING

Write a story about going with a friend to a special street in another town. Tell what happens. Be sure to use special nouns.

Grade 2: Unit 3 Nouns and Pronouns *(Use with pupil book pages 105–106.)*
Skill: Students will write proper nouns correctly. They will write an original story.

Name ______________________

7 Pronouns

Nouns	Pronouns
The attic is messy.	**It** is messy.
Dad moves boxes.	**He** moves boxes.
Mom helps.	**She** helps.
Dad and Mom work hard.	**They** work hard.

Write the pronoun that can take the place of the underlined word or words in each sentence. Use the words from the Word Box to help you.

It	He	She	They

1. Carlos and Jane are having a yard sale. ______________
2. The yard sale was Carlos's idea. ______________
3. Carlos wanted to clean the attic. ______________
4. Jane wanted to clean the basement. ______________
5. The basement is clean now. ______________
6. Mom and Dad are proud. ______________

Name ______________________________

7 Pronouns (continued from page 39)

Challenge

Write the pronouns that can take the place of the underlined word or words in each sentence. Then write the pronouns in the puzzle.

1. Carlos and Jane are in the attic. ______________
2. Carlos has found a box. ______________
3. The box is big. ______________
4. Jane looks inside. ______________

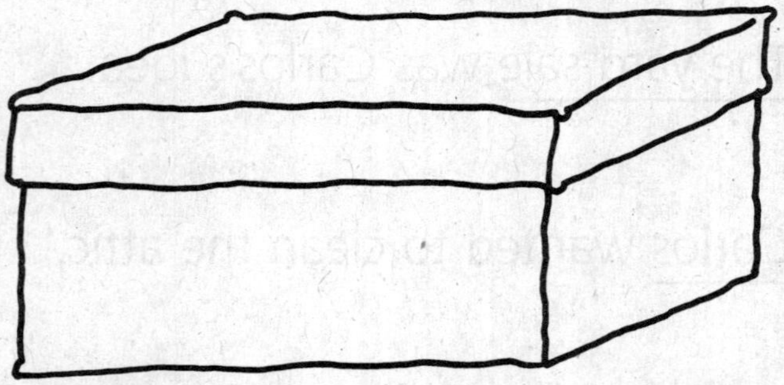

Writing Application: Sentences

DESCRIBING

Suppose that you clean out your attic and find some old pictures. Write sentences about what the people are doing in the pictures. Use the pronouns he, she, it, and they.

Grade 2: Unit 3 Nouns and Pronouns *(Use with pupil book pages 107–108.)*
Skill: Students will use pronouns correctly. They will write original sentences.

Name ______________________________

Writing Clearly with Nouns and Pronouns

With nouns:	**The flowers** are on the table. **The flowers** are in the bowl.
With pronouns:	**The flowers** are on the table. **They** are in the bowl.

Using Pronouns 1-5. Find the sentences with naming parts that are repeated. Use a pronoun in place of one of the naming parts. Write the new paragraph.

Grandma has a nice garden. Grandma works in it every day. Uncle Dave mows the lawn on Sunday. Uncle Dave rakes the leaves. Lila helps pull the weeds. Lila trims the bushes. The robins use the birdbath. The robins eat the worms. Mom and Dad like this garden. Mom and Dad started a garden, too.

Name ______________________________

Writing Clearly with Nouns and Pronouns

With nouns:	**Paula and Rob** were outside. **Paula and Rob** took a walk.
With pronouns:	**Paula and Rob** were outside. **They** took a walk.

Using Pronouns Find the sentences with naming parts that are repeated. Use a pronoun in place of one of the naming parts. Write the new sentence.

Marc likes to ski. Marc goes skiing with his family. The skis are new. The skis are bright and shiny. Marc and his dad ski together. Marc and his dad have fun. Skiing is not hard to learn. Skiing is a great sport.

1. ______________________________

2. ______________________________

3. ______________________________

4. ______________________________

Grade 2: Unit 3 Nouns and Pronouns *(Use with pupil book pages 109–110.)*
Skill: Students will replace nouns with pronouns and write new sentences.

Name ____________________

8 Naming Yourself Last

Ann and I have fun in the kitchen.
Daniel and I like shopping for food.

A Write the words from the Word Box to finish each sentence.

Luis	I

1. ____________ **and** ____________ baked bread.

Lori	I

2. ____________ **and** ____________ made soup.

B **3–5.** Proofread this part of a diary Find three mistakes using I. Correct each mistake.

Example ~~I~~ and ~~Hakim~~ went to the store. (Hakim ... I)

Proofreading

Joy and I bought apples. I and Laney chose some corn. Then I and Frank bought beans. After that, I and Hakim made lunch.

Name ______________________________

8 Naming Yourself Last (continued from page 43)

Challenge

Color the vegetables that have correct sentences. Write the other sentences correctly.

Carlo and I pick pumpkins.

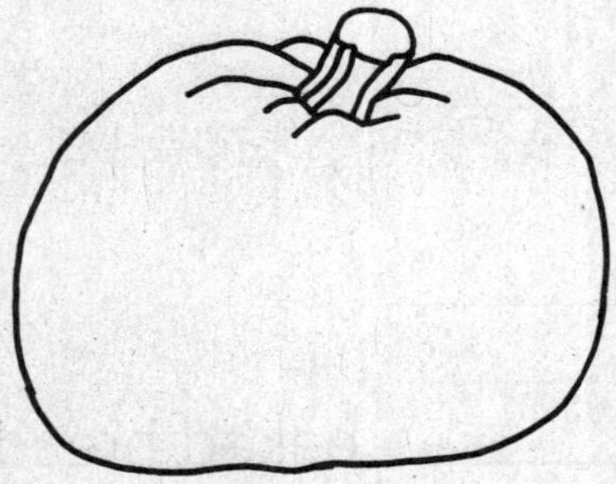

I and Mom chop carrots.

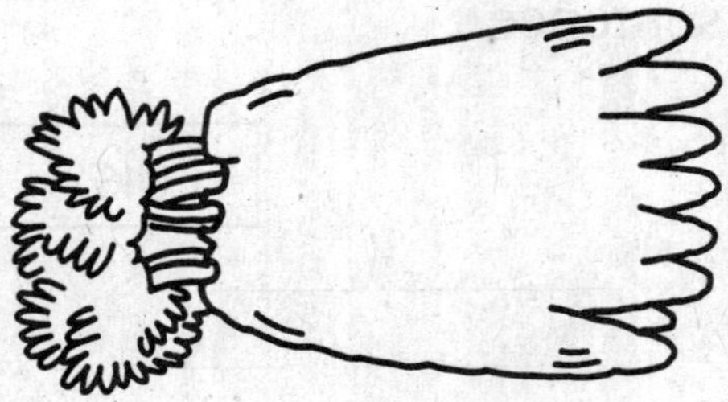

I and Jed love corn.

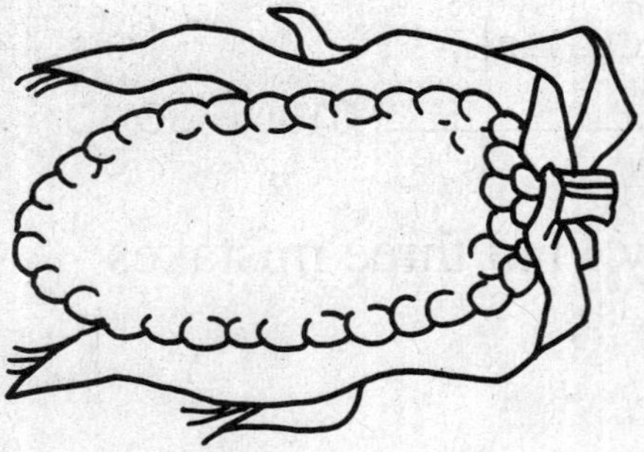

Dad and I wash a green pepper.

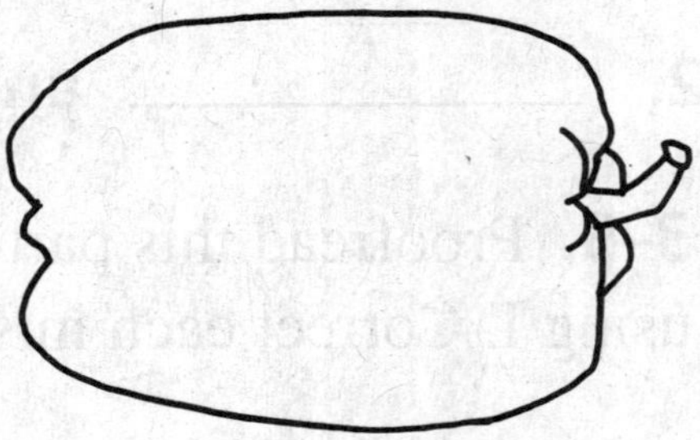

1. ______________________________

2. ______________________________

Writing Application: Sentences

INFORMING

Write sentences about foods that you and a friend like to eat. Use your friend's name and the word I.

Name ______________________________

9 Nouns Ending with 's

Laura's cat	Danny's mouse
Karen's rat	Devin's house

A Draw a line under each noun that correctly shows ownership.

1. Nira's fish swims all day.

Niras fish swims all day.

2. The cats food is outside.

The cat's food is outside.

B **3–6.** Proofread this part of a news story. Find four nouns that should be changed to show ownership.

Example ~~Eileens~~ Eileen's hamster eats a lot.

Proofreading

John Barber's dog left home today. It dug up Ben Smiths garden. It then ran after Lucy Blues cats. Later, it broke Mr. Eddys door. The dogs barks were heard all over town.

Name ______________________________

9 Nouns Ending with 's (continued from page 45)

Challenge

Read Jim's letter. Rewrite the underlined nouns to show ownership.

Dear Lois,

My kitten name is Roger. He likes to eat our dog food.

______________________ ______________________

Roger plays with my sister hair. At night he sleeps on Brian

______________________ ______________________

bed. In the morning he sleeps in my mom garden. Tell me

____

about your pets.

Your friend,

Jerry

Writing Application: Nouns Ending with 's

INFORMING

Write a sentence about something that belongs to a pet.

____

Grade 2: Unit 3 Nouns and Pronouns *(Use with pupil book pages 113–114.)*
Skill: Students will write possessive nouns that end in *'s*. They will write an original sentence.

Name ______________________

10 Nouns Ending with s'

girls' bikes	boys' hats
dogs' food	friends' flowers

A Draw a line under each noun that shows ownership correctly.

1. two cousin's maps
   two cousins' maps
2. three mothers' cars
   three mother's cars

B Write each underlined noun correctly.

3. the three uncles sons ______________
4. my two aunts dresses ______________
5. five brothers hats ______________
6. six sisters rings ______________
7. four fathers cars ______________
8. two grandmother's pies ______________

Name ___________________________________

10 Nouns Ending with s' (continued from page 47)

Challenge

Jean took a picture at the beach. Find four things that people have or own. Then write these things on the lines.
Hint: You can use these words: wings, sails, bones, buckets

Here is one to get you started.

Example. boys hats boys' hats

1. ______________________ 3. ______________________

2. ______________________ 4. ______________________

Writing Application: Nouns Ending with s' NARRATING

Write a story about playing a game with friends. Use two nouns that name more than one that show ownership.

Grade 2: Unit 3 Nouns and Pronouns *(Use with pupil book pages 115–116.)*
Skill: Students will write possessive nouns that end in *s'*. They will write an original story.

Name ____________________

Exact Nouns

kitchen pots
This room is full of things.

Revising 1-5. Change each underlined noun to a more exact noun. Choose words from the word box.

apples	painter	green beans	cats	statues
lamps	babies	shoes	robot	roses

Revising

My cousin Julio is a worker. He likes to paint pictures of people. Sometimes, Julio draws pictures of fruit. Other times, he paints pictures of flowers. He also likes to draw colorful pictures of animals. I like to watch Julio work. His paintings are beautiful.

Name ______________________

Choosing a Problem

Problem: Theo the cat needs a new home for his family.

Solution: Friendly birds fly over town and find Theo's family a nice warm barn.

Read the main character and setting. Complete the chart by listing two problems for the main character. List one way the character could solve each problem.

Main Character: a mouse **Setting:** a boat in the ocean

Problem 1: **Solution:**
Problem 2: **Solution:**

Grade 2: Unit 4 Story *(Use with pupil book page 145.)*
Skill: Students will complete a problem and solution chart for a given character and setting.

Name ______________________________

Developing Characters

Daisy the Lamb

happy eats daisies black and fluffy

Draw a picture of a story character. Complete the web with details about the character. Tell what the character looks like, how he or she feels and thinks, and what he or she does.

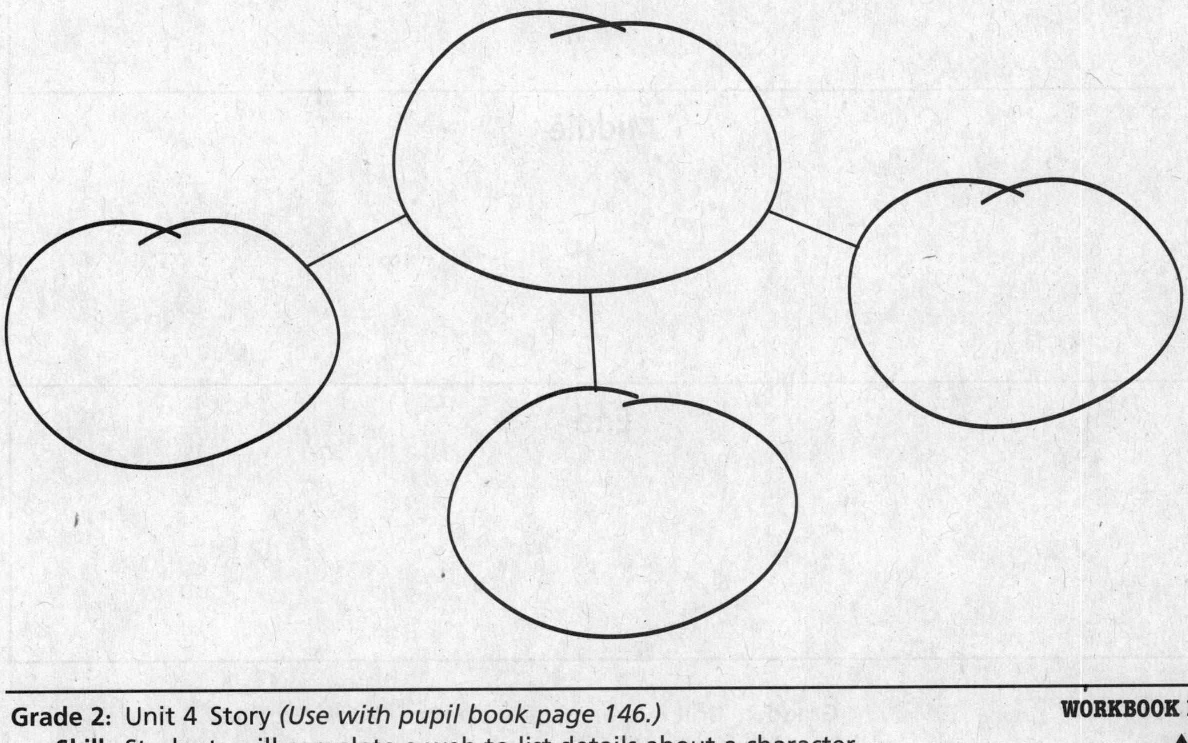

Name ______________________________

Mapping Your Story

Beginning	Middle	End
Little Red Riding Hood	meets mean wolf	woodsman saves her

Think about a story you know well. Write the name of the story.

____

Complete the story map with events from the story. Write the story events in order.

Beginning
Middle
End

Grade 2: Unit 4 Story *(Use with pupil book page 147.)*
Skill: Students will complete a story map for a well-known story.

Name ______________________________

Beginning Your Story

Weak Beginning	Strong Beginning
This story is about Jamie. Last week was Jamie's birthday.	When Jamie woke, he was already smiling. Can you imagine the best day of your life?

What beginning would you write for a story about a boy who suddenly became invisible? Write two different beginnings for the story. Check the one you like better.

☐ **1.** ______________________________

☐ **2.** ______________________________

Name ______________________________

Revising a Story

Have I	yes
• added details about the character and setting?	☐
• written a clear beginning, middle, and end?	☐
• written an interesting beginning?	☐

Revise this story to make it better. Check off each box when you have finished revising. Write your changes in the spaces above each line, on the sides, and below the paragraph.

The boy's name was Ramón. He lived in a big house with his mother and sister. When his best friend, Robert, moved to Seattle, Ramón felt lonely. He asked his sister what to do. She did not know. He asked his mother what to do. She said, "Well, maybe we could get you a puppy to keep you company."

Grade 2: Unit 4 Story *(Use with pupil book page 149.)*
Skill: Students will revise a story, using a checklist as a guide.

Name ____________________

Revising Strategies: Sentence Fluency

swiftly
The owl flew ^ over the field.

quickly
The mouse ran ^ under the bush.

Add an adverb to each sentence to tell how the action was done.

1. The wind blew.

2. The animals waited.

3. The moon rose.

4. The horses raced.

5. The frog croaked.

Name ______________________

1 Verbs

Erik **ties** his dog Snowy to his sled.

Write the verb in each sentence.

1. Eric sits on the sled. ______________
2. The dogs stand in front. ______________
3. The sleds race. ______________
4. Erik calls to the dogs. ______________
5. The dogs run ahead. ______________
6. Erik holds the ropes. ______________
7. The sled crosses the line. ______________
8. Erik yells loudly. ______________

Grade 2: Unit 5 Verbs *(Use with pupil book pages 163–164.)*
Skill: Students will identify and write verbs.

Grammar

Name ______________________________

1 Verbs (continued from page 56)

Challenge

Find the verb in the Word Box that goes with each picture clue. Write the verb in the puzzle.

laugh	hop	plant	shake	sit	eat

ACROSS

Example

1. laugh

3. ______________

5. ______________

DOWN

2. ______________

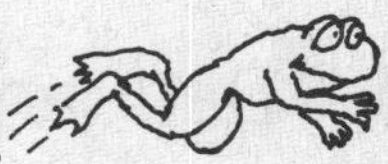

3. ______________

4. ______________

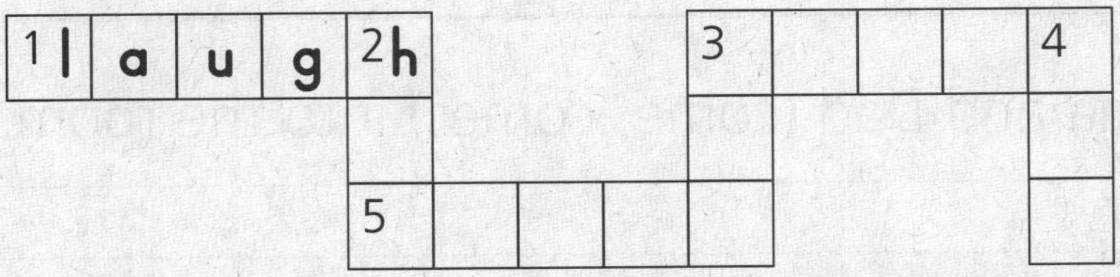

Writing Application: A Story

NARRATING

Write a story about a dog that can talk and fly. Try to use a different verb in each sentence. Circle the verbs.

Name ______________________

2 Verbs That Tell About Now

Dad **makes** breakfast.

The girls **make** breakfast.

Write the sentences correctly.

1. Dad (answer, answers) the doorbell.

2. Kim (feed, feeds) her egg to the dog.

3. Nina (pour, pours) milk on the table.

4. Grandma and Dad (come, comes) into the room.

5. The girls (clean, cleans) the kitchen.

Grade 2: Unit 5 Verbs *(Use with pupil book pages 165–166.)*
Skill: Students will choose present-tense verbs that agree with their subjects.

Name ________________________________

2 Verbs That Tell About Now (continued from page 58)

Challenge

Tammy wants her big brother Marty to read to her. He reads a book about animals. Choose a verb from the Word Box to finish each sentence. Then write the letters that are in the squares on the line below to spell a secret word.

eat	digs	runs	leap

1. The horse [ ] ___ ___ ___ fast.
2. Cows [ ] ___ ___ grass.
3. The frogs ___ ___ [ ] ___ over each other.
4. The dog [ ] ___ ___ ___.

The secret word is ________________________________.

Writing Application: Sentences

DESCRIBING

Suppose that you have little brothers and sisters. Write sentences telling what they do. Be sure to use verbs that tell about now.

Name ____________________________________

3 Pronouns and Verbs

He runs the race.	**They run** the race.
I fix the bike.	**She fixes** the bike.
You ride the bike.	**We ride** the bikes.

A Draw a line under each correct sentence.

1. They rides fast.

They ride fast.

2. She pedals hard.

She pedal hard.

3. I win the race!

I wins the race!

B **4–6.** Proofread this part of a radio report. Find two verbs that should match their pronouns. Correct each mistake.

Example They ~~leaves~~ leave the city today.

Proofreading

Five trains aren't running today. "They stopped at nine o'clock," says Mr. Jordan. He say that this problem will make a lot of people late. They rides to work on the trains.

Grade 2: Unit 5 Verbs *(Use with pupil book pages 167–168.)*
Skill: Students will identify correct pronouns and verbs. Students will correct errors in pronouns and verbs.

Name ______________________

3 Pronouns and Verbs (continued from page 60)

Challenge

Read Jerry's post card. He made some mistakes with pronouns and verbs. Rewrite the post card correctly.

Dear Sasha,

We are on a train! It make a lot of noise. I know you likes to ride on trains. I loves it. Anna is very happy on the train. She send her love to you.

Your cousin,

Jerry

1. ______________________
2. ______________________
3. ______________________
4. ______________________

Writing Application: Pronouns and Verbs — NARRATING

Write a story about going on a bus, train, or airplane. Use two examples of pronouns and verbs.

Name ______________________

4 Verbs with ed

Now the students **wait**.

Yesterday the students **waited**.

Write each sentence. Make the underlined verb show that something happened in the past.

1. Rachel listen to each word.

2. Mrs. Lopez call Rachel's word.

3. Rachel whisper the word.

4. She remember the word.

5. Rachel print her word on the board.

6. She spell her word correctly!

Grade 2: Unit 5 Verbs *(Use with pupil book pages 169–170.)*
Skill: Students will form the past tense of regular verbs.

Name ______________________________

4 Verbs with ed (continued from page 63)

Challenge

Emily wrote a letter to her friend Tom. She used verbs that tell about now. Write Emily's letter, using verbs that tell about the past. Use another sheet of paper.

Dear Tom,

Last week in school, we watch a movie about whales. I paint a picture of a whale. Sarah and I learn our times tables. I spell all of the words correctly on my spelling test. On Tuesday we play ball outside. We start a new game. Liz and Tony jump high for the ball. We rest after the game.

Your friend,

Emily

Writing Application: Sentences

INFORMING

Write sentences to tell about something you did when you were in the first grade. Use verbs that end with ed.

Name ______________________________

Combining Sentences: Action Parts

Two sentences:	My brother **cooks**.
	My brother **bakes**.
One sentence:	My brother **cooks** and **bakes**.

Joining Action Parts 1-4. Read each underlined sentence pair. Join the action parts. Write the new paragraph.

He will bake a big cake. He will frost it. Jana will pour the juice. Jana will serve the cake. Mom will laugh. Mom will smile at us. She will taste her cake. She will enjoy her birthday party. We'll all have a great time!

Grade 2: Unit 5 Verbs (*Use with pupil book pages 171–172.*)
Skill: Students will join action parts to combine sentences.

Name ______________________________

Combining Sentences: Action Parts

Two sentences:	Laura sings very well. Laura dances nicely.
One sentence:	Laura **sings very well** and **dances nicely**.

Joining Action Parts Read each underlined sentence pair. Join the naming parts. Write the new sentences.

The thunder was booming. The thunder was crashing. Lightning flashed in my eyes. Lightning scared the dog. This was a bad storm. It flooded the street. It blew down trees. The rain made huge puddles. The rain ran down the street. I was glad when it was over.

1. ______________________________

2. ______________________________

3. ______________________________

4. ______________________________

Name ______________________________

5 ran, run and came, come

Karen **ran** a mile in ten minutes.
Jake **has run** a mile in less time.

Charlie **came** to the race.
Mom and Terry **have come** too.

Write each sentence correctly.

1. A large crowd (came, come) to the race.

2. Maggie and I have (came, come) early.

3. We (ran, run) all the way.

4. The runners have (came, come) to the line.

5. Nick has (ran, run) in the race before.

Grade 2: Unit 5 Verbs (*Use with pupil book pages 173-174.*)
Skill: Students will use *ran*, *run*, *came*, and *come* correctly.

Name ______________________

5 ran, run and came, come (continued from page 66)

Challenge

Lola took a picture of her school's race. Tell what is happening in the picture. Write four sentences. Use ran, run, came, or come in each sentence.

1. ______________________

2. ______________________

3. ______________________

4. ______________________

Writing Application: A Story

NARRATING

Write a story about a make-believe race. You could have animals, famous people, or your friends in your race. Use the verbs ran, run, came, and come.

Name ______________________________

6 saw, seen and went, gone

Jeff **saw** the beach from his house.
He **has seen** many beautiful sunsets.
Jeff **went** to his bedroom window.
The sun **has gone** down.

A Write each sentence correctly.

1. Jeff and I (went, gone) to the beach.

____

2. Sometimes Jeff has (saw, seen) some crabs.

____

B **3–5.** Proofread this part of an article. Find four errors using saw, seen and went, gone. Correct each mistake.

Example Jeff ~~seen~~ saw lots of birds.

Proofreading

Jeff seen thousands of birds each year. He gone all over to find them. He had went many places to watch birds. People have saw him early in the morning watching the birds.

Name ______________________________

6 saw, seen and went, gone (continued from page 68)

Challenge

Jan left this note for her mother. She did not use saw, seen, went, and gone correctly. Write the note correctly.

> Alex and I have went to the store. He has saw a book about the sea. He has went there for it. I gone to the cleaners for you. I seen Mrs. Black there.

Writing Application: Sentences

DESCRIBING

Write four sentences about a place that you like to visit. Use the words saw and seen in two sentences. Use the words went and gone in two sentences.

Name ______________________________

7 did, done and gave, given

My family **did** a nice thing.
We **have done** things for people before.
We **gave** Grandmother a party.
Grandfather **has given** her a present.

Write each sentence correctly.

1. We (gave, given) many gifts.

2. Then everyone (did, done) something special.

3. Dad (did, done) a funny dance.

4. He has (did, done) this dance before.

5. Everyone has (gave, given) him a cheer.

Grade 2: Unit 5 Verbs *(Use with pupil book pages 177–178.)*
Skill: Students will use *did*, *done*, *gave*, and *given* correctly.

Name ______________________

7 did, done and gave, given (continued from page 70)

Challenge

Mr. Russell is writing an ad for Russell's Store. Help him write it correctly. Find the verb that is not correct in each sentence. Then write the ad correctly. Add a sentence of your own to the ad. Use did, done, gave, or given.

> Russell's Store has gave great sales before.
>
> This year we done it again.
>
> We have gave you the best sale ever!

Writing Application: Sentences — INFORMING

Write at least four sentences about a party. Tell about a gift that was given. Use the words did, done, gave, and given.

Name ____________________

8 is and are

The storm **is** over at last.

The children **are** outside in the yard.

A Write each sentence correctly.

1. The winds (is, are) gone now.

2. Many branches (is, are) broken.

3. The birdbath (is, are) full of rainwater.

B **4–7.** Proofread this part of a traffic report. Find four errors with is and are. Correct each mistake.

Example The car ~~are~~ is off the road.

Proofreading

There are a traffic jam on Highway 29. Some trees is down from the storm. Cars is stopped going both ways. The storm are gone. The traffic is still bad.

Grade 2: Unit 5 Verbs *(Use with pupil book pages 179–180.)*
Skill: Students will use *is* and *are* correctly.

Name ______________________________

8 is and are (continued from page 72)

Challenge

Look at the picture. Write a story about the picture. Use the words is and are.

____

____

____

____

Writing Application: Sentences

DESCRIBING

Write four sentences about playing in the rain. Use the words is and are.

Name ____________________

9 was and were

> Pedro **was** wide awake.
>
> His two brothers **were** asleep.

A Write each sentence correctly.

1. The night sky (was, were) black.

____

2. Soon Pedro (was, were) tired.

____

B **3–6.** Proofread this part of a poem. It has four errors using was and were. Correct each mistake.

Example Pedro ~~were~~ was saying this poem.

Proofreading

The stars was out, the moon were bright.
The boys and girls was tucked in tight.
And up above a shooting star
Were flying, flying oh so far.

Name ______________________________

9 was and were (continued from page 74)

(continued from page 74)

Challenge

Write was or were to finish the first four sentences of this story. Then write two sentences of your own to finish the story. Use was and were in your sentences.

The thunder __________ loud. The lightning __________ very close. Suddenly the house __________ dark. All the lights __________ out! ______________________________

____

____

Writing Application: A Sentence

DESCRIBING

Have you ever played or camped outside at night? Write two sentences about being outside in the dark. Use was in one sentence. Use were in the other sentence.

Name ______________________

10 Contractions

do not	**don't**	does not	**doesn't**
is not	**isn't**	cannot	**can't**

A Write the correct contraction.

1. Arnold is not happy. ____________

2. He cannot find his glasses. ____________

3. His glasses do not often get lost. ____________

4. He does not see them on his head! ____________

B **5–8.** Proofread these newspaper headlines. Find four contractions that are not correct. Correct each mistake.

Example Boy ~~Cant~~ Can't Find Glasses

Proofreading

Bus Line Doesnt Run

People Cant Get to Work

Lost Monkey Isnt Found

Police Dont Know Where He Is

Grade 2: Unit 5 Verbs *(Use with pupil book pages 183–184.)*
Skill: Students will form contractions for *do not*, *does not*, *is not*, and *cannot*.

Name ____________________

10 Contractions (continued from page 76)

Challenge

Help Tony and Lola's mom write a note to explain why Tony and Lola are late for school today. Replace the underlined words in the note with the correct contraction from the Word Box. Write the note.

did not	didn't	was not	wasn't
were not	weren't	we are	we're

Dear Mrs. Moore,

Our clock did not ring this morning. It was not plugged in! Tony and Lola were not able to catch the bus. We are sorry.

____

____

____

____

Writing Application: Sentences

DESCRIBING

Write four sentences about something that you have lost. Use the contractions don't, doesn't, isn't, and can't.

Name ____________________

Exact Verbs

raced handed

We <u>went</u> to the gate and <u>gave</u> the man our tickets.

Revising 1-5. Change each underlined verb to a more exact verb. Use words from the word box. Cross out the weak verb and write the exact verb over it.

cracked	strolled	stared	caught	saw
dashed	hurled	slept	creep	tossed

Revising

The Sports Fair was about to begin. We were excited. First, we <u>looked</u> as a skater did flips. Then we <u>went</u> over to the baseball area. I <u>threw</u> the ball very fast! Next, I <u>walked</u> to the basketball court. I tried to make some baskets, but then I just <u>put</u> the ball aside. We really like going to Sports Fair and trying new things.

Grade 2: Unit 5 Verbs (*Use with pupil book page 185.*)
Skill: Students will revise sentences by choosing exact verbs.

Name ____________________

Using Order Words

Order Words			
first	second	third	last
next	finally	then	now

Look at the pictures. Choose an order word for each step. Write the order word and the step in the chart.

Order Word	Step

Name ______________________________

Topic Sentence

Weak Topic Sentence	Strong Topic Sentence
Here's how to break an egg.	Sometimes you have to break an egg. Here's how to do it right.

Write a strong topic sentence for these instructions.

____

____

____

First, have a grown-up help you cut off the top of a carrot. Next, take three toothpicks and stick them into the side of the carrot top. Then, fill a plastic cup with water. Now, put the carrot top into the cup so the toothpicks rest on the edges and the carrot piece sticks into the water. Wait a few days and you will see roots start to grow. Last, green leaves will grow out of the top.

Grade 2: Unit 6 Instructions *(Use with pupil book page 215.)*
Skill: Students will write a strong topic sentence.

Name ______________________________

Revising Instructions

Have I	yes
• written an interesting topic sentence?	☐
• included all the steps and written them in order?	☐
• used order words such as first, next, then, and finally?	☐

Revise these instructions. Check off each box when you have finished your changes. Write your changes in the spaces above each line, on the sides, and below the paragraph.

You can make a picture post card for a friend. First, take a regular index card. Next, glue the picture to the plain side of the index card. Then, cut out a pretty magazine picture. Now, write a message on the left half of the lined side. Write your friend's address on the other half. Stamp your post card and drop it in the mailbox.

Name ______________________

Revising Strategies: Word Choice

skipped
We ~~went~~ across the field in the warm sun.

Read each sentence. Then choose an exact verb to replace each underlined verb. Write the new sentence.

1. First, <u>make</u> some strips of colored paper.

2. Next, <u>make</u> one into a circle and tape the ends together.

3. Then, <u>put</u> another strip through the first circle and tape those ends together.

4. After all the strips are used, <u>put</u> the ends together to make a pretty wreath.

Name ______________________________

1 Adjectives: How Things Look

Size:	This is a **huge** plant.
Shape:	It has **flat** leaves.
Color:	The blossoms are **purple** and **pink**.
How Many:	There are **six** flowers on the plant.

Write the adjective from the Word Box that best fits each sentence.

one	three	round	red	small

1. Martin grows flowers in ________________ boxes.
   (how many)

2. The flowers in ________________ box are all white.
   (how many)

3. Martin waters his ________________ plants first.
   (size)

4. Martin fills a ________________ pot with soil.
   (shape)

5. The soil is for the plant with ________________ leaves.
   (color)

Name ______________________________

1 Adjectives: How Things Look (continued from page 83)

Challenge

Read the clues for the puzzle. Each answer is an adjective. Write the answers in the puzzle.

ACROSS

2. thin

6. sunny color

7. not many

8. almost ten

9. pancake shape

DOWN

1. lots

3. thick

4. sky color

5. ball shape

7. mouse size

Writing Application: Sentences

DESCRIBING

Write four sentences that describe flowers and plants. Use adjectives that tell size, shape, color, and how many.

Grade 2: Unit 7 Adjectives *(Use with pupil book pages 239–240.)*
Skill: Students will use adjectives that describe size, shape, color, and number.

Name ____________________

2 Adjectives: Taste and Smell

Taste: I make **sweet** juice for Mom.
Smell: Mom smells the **fresh** flowers.

Write the word that describes the underlined word in each sentence.

1. Mom loves the fresh smell of daisies. ____________
2. Mom tastes the peppery eggs. ____________
3. She likes the taste of spicy food. ____________
4. The toast I made smells burnt. ____________
5. Mom says the juice tastes sweet. ____________
6. She loves the creamy milk. ____________
7. I like sour lemons. ____________
8. Dad cooks tasty oatmeal. ____________

Name ______________________________

2 Adjectives: Taste and Smell (continued from page 85)

Challenge

Todd and his family are cooking some fish on the beach. Help them describe their food. Find the word from the Word Box that completes each sentence. Write each word in the puzzle.

salty	fishy	sour	sweet	smoky	spicy

ACROSS

1. The fire smells __?__.
4. The seawater tastes __?__.

DOWN

1. We put a hot sauce that tastes __?__ on the fish.
2. The lemon on the fish tastes __?__.
3. The fish dinner smells __?__.
4. The corn tastes __?__.

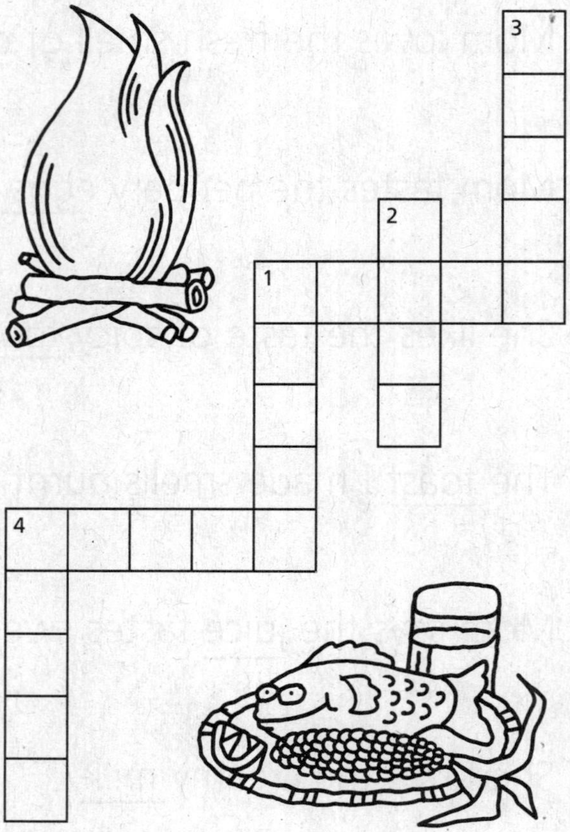

Writing Application: An Ad

EXPLAINING

Make up a new food. Think about how it tastes and smells. Write an ad to tell how your food tastes and smells.

Grade 2: Unit 7 Adjectives (*Use with pupil book pages 241–242.*)
Skill: Students will identify adjectives that describe taste and smell. They will write an original advertisement.

Name ______________________

3 Adjectives: Sound and Texture

Sound: Some birds make a **tapping** noise.

Feel: Their beaks must be very **sharp**.

Use an adjective from the Word Box to complete each sentence.

flapping	splashing	soft
light	humming	oily

1. This bird makes a ______________ sound.

2. It makes a ______________ sound in water.

3. It feels very ______________ in my hand.

4. The feathers are ______________.

5. Some birds' feathers feel ______________.

6. The wings make a ______________ sound.

Grammar · Name ______________________

3 Adjectives: Sound and Texture (continued from page 87)

Challenge

Help Annie match adjectives with these pictures. Write an adjective from the basket to describe each picture.

1. ______________ ice

4. a ______________ friend

2. ______________ waves

5. a ______________ iron

3. a ______________ day

6. a ______________ door

Writing Application: Sentences

DESCRIBING

Write two sentences about a bird or other animal. Tell how it sounds and how it feels.

Grade 2: Unit 7 Adjectives (*Use with pupil book pages 243–244.*)
Skill: Students will use adjectives that describe sound and touch. They will write original sentences.

Name ______________________________

Expanding Sentences: Adjectives

Without adjectives: This is my coat.
With adjectives: This is my **gray** coat.

Using Adjectives to Tell More 1-5. Read each underlined sentence. Use the adjective in ( ) to tell more. Write the new paragraph.

My mom and I went shopping. We both bought clothes. (new) Mom found a scarf. (purple) I got slippers. (fuzzy) Then we stopped for some soup. (tasty) Mom and I enjoyed our day. (great) It was lots of fun.

Name ______________________________

Expanding Sentences: Adjectives

Without adjectives:	The clouds floated in the sky.
With adjectives:	The **fluffy** clouds floated in the **blue** sky.

Using Adjectives to Tell More Read each underlined sentence. Use an adjective from the word box to tell more. Write the new sentences.

tasty	heavy	warm	soft

The sun shone down on the park. I was ready for the picnic. I had the bag with the juice. My brother had the blankets to sit on. Dad had the cookies that he always bakes. The grass looked cool and green. I couldn't wait to take a nap on it.

1. ______________________________

2. ______________________________

3. ______________________________

4. ______________________________

Skill: Students will expand sentences by adding adjectives.

Name ______________________

4 Using a and an

a fish	**a** mouse
an eagle	**an** otter

A Write each group of words correctly.

1. an cow ______ a owl ______

2. a ostrich ______ an beaver ______

B **3–6.** Proofread this part of an encyclopedia article. Find four places to fix a or an. Correct each mistake.

Example ~~A~~ An eagle can fly.

Proofreading

Animals That Can Fly

An bird can fly. A insect can fly. An bat can fly. An Arctic tern flies 22,000 miles in a year! A insect's wings beat more than 1,000 times each second.

Name ____________________

4 Using a and an (continued from page 91)

Challenge

Sally Squirrel lives in the forest. She has lots of friends. Who do you see? Use a or an to complete the sentences about Sally's friends. You can use these animals: otter, mouse, owl, fox, and bird.

I see ____________________ on the ground.

I see ____________________ in the air.

I see ____________________ on a branch.

I see ____________________ in the creek.

I see ____________________ under ground.

Writing Application: a and an — INFORMING

Write three sentences about animals that fly. Use a and an at least one time each.

Name ______________________________

5 Adjectives with er and est

A Write the correct word to finish each sentence.

1. Our pond is ____________________ than the lake.
   (warmer, warmest)

2. The sea is ____________________ than the lake.
   (cooler, coolest)

B **3–6.** Proofread this part of a report. Find four places to change er and est. Correct each mistake.

Example Pine Lake is the ~~larger~~ largest lake of all.

Proofreading

Pine Lake is deepest than Blue Lake. Lake Silver is the deeper lake of all. The trees around Lake Silver are tallest than the trees at Pine Lake. Blue Lake has the colder water of all.

Name ____________________

5 Adjectives with <u>er</u> and <u>est</u> (continued from page 93)

Challenge

Joel is spending a week at camp. Help Joel write a letter to his parents. Write the underlined words correctly.

> Dear Mom and Dad,
>
> The air seems <u>fresh</u> here than it does at home. The nights are <u>quiet</u> than at home too. My bed here is <u>hard</u> than my bed back home. I think my bed is the <u>hard</u> bed of all the beds here! The cabin is the <u>dark</u> place I have ever been.
>
> Love, Joel

Example fresh fresher

1. ____________________

2. ____________________.

3. ____________________

4. ____________________

Writing Application: A Story

NARRATING

Write a story about a strange land. Everything is a different size, shape, or color. Use adjectives with <u>er</u> and <u>est</u> to describe the things you find in the strange land.

Name ______________________________

Combining Sentences: Adjectives

Two sentences:	This fish is **small**. This fish is **shiny**.
One sentence:	This fish is **small** and **shiny**.

Joining Sentences with Adjectives 1-4. Read the underlined sentence pairs. Join the sentences using and between the adjectives. Write the new paragraph.

I have a fish tank with lots of fish. The tank is big. The tank is heavy. The fish food is soft. The fish food is flaky. I keep the water clear. I keep the water warm. These fish dash. These fish dart. They are very lively to watch.

Name ______________________________

Combining Sentences: Adjectives

Two sentences:	My piggy bank is **big**. My piggy bank is **pink**.
One sentence:	My piggy bank is **big** and **pink**.

Joining Sentences with Adjectives Read the underlined sentence pairs. Join the sentences using and between the adjectives. Write the new sentences.

The money in my bank is shiny. The money in my bank is jingly. I will buy something big. I will buy something soft. The toy I buy will be brown. The toy I buy will be white. The toy I buy will have shoes. The toy I buy will have a hat. The toy I buy will keep me company at night. It is a teddy bear!

1. ______________________________

2. ______________________________

3. ______________________________

4. ______________________________

Grade 2: Unit 7 Adjectives (*Use with pupil book pages 251–252.*)
Skill: Students will combine sentences by joining adjectives.

Name ______________________

Antonyms

See the **bright** moon in the **dark** sky.

Revising 1-4. Change each underlined word to an antonym. Use words from the word box. Cross out the word and write the antonym over it.

larger	green	fast	bigger
warm	wet	soft	yellow

Revising

The night was <u>cool</u> and clear. We sat on the <u>hard</u> ground and watched the stars. There was a <u>small</u> star next to the moon. I thought it was a planet. Then it seemed to get <u>tinier</u>. It wasn't a planet. It was the lights of a plane!

Name ______________________________

Using Your Senses

Taste	Smell	See	Hear	Feel
sweet	burnt	bright	loud	sandy
salty	fresh	neat	quiet	fluffy
sour	flowery	yellow	crackling	smooth

Choose a topic from the list below. Write the topic in the chart. Complete the chart. List and describe what you observe using your senses.

an apple   a playground   a city street   new pajamas

Five Senses Chart
My Topic:
See
Smell
Taste
Hear
Feel

Grade 2: Unit 8 Description *(Use with pupil book page 275.)*
Skill: Students will complete a chart to describe sensory details.

Name ______________________________

Writing Similes

Her eyes twinkled like stars.

The grass was as green as emeralds.

Think about an object in your kitchen at home. Then write two sentences that compare the object to something else. Use your five senses to help you. Remember to use as or like in your sentences.

1. ______________________________

2. ______________________________

Name ______________________________

Topic Sentence

Weak Topic Sentence: The toy was old.

Strong Topic Sentence: The toy was an old bear that played a drum.

Write two strong topic sentences for the description below. Circle the one you like better.

The clock is painted with leaves and flowers. One flower is a blooming rose. Every hour, the chimes make bell sounds. They play a tune like a music box. Best of all, when the hands point to twelve o'clock, a little bird comes out of a door.

Topic Sentence 1 ______________________________

____

____

Topic Sentence 2 ______________________________

____

____

Grade 2: Unit 8 Description *(Use with pupil book page 278.)*
Skill: Students will write strong topic sentences for a description and circle the best one.

Name ____________________

Revising a Description

Have I	yes
• written about one thing, place, or event?	☐
• written a clear and interesting topic sentence?	☐
• used my senses to help list details?	☐
• used adjectives and similes in my description?	☐

Revise this description to make it better. Check off each box to be sure. You can write your changes in the spaces above each line, on the sides, and below the paragraph.

I like Yosemite Park. There are trees and waterfalls. The waterfalls look nice. The air smells fresh and clean. Yosemite is a valley with rock walls. Thousands of people visit it every year. Yellowstone is also nice. In the summer, Yosemite is full of visitors taking pictures. There are a lot of beautiful sights.

Name ______________________

Revising Strategies: Sentence Fluency

older   slippery
My ^ sister came down the ^ stairs.

Add one or two adjectives to each sentence to describe the underlined nouns.

1. The apple was on the table.

2. The campfire lit our faces.

3. A bird landed on the branch.

4. The man saw a fox.

5. The squirrel ate the nut.

Grade 2: Unit 8 Description *(Use with pupil book page 282.)*
Skill: Students will add adjectives to revise sentences.

Name ______________________

1 Days

Chris will pick berries on Saturday.

Write the day of the week to finish each sentence about Chris's week. Use the chart to find the correct days.

Monday	Tuesday	Wednesday	Thursday	Friday
clean my room	club meeting	softball practice	study for test	movie with Gram

1. On ______________ Chris will see a movie.

2. Chris will study for a test on ______________.

3. On ______________ Chris has softball practice.

4. Chris will clean her room on ______________.

5. On ______________ Chris has a club meeting.

Name ______________________________

1 Days (continued from page 103)

Challenge

Read the clues for the puzzle.
Each answer is a noun.
Write the answers in
the puzzle.

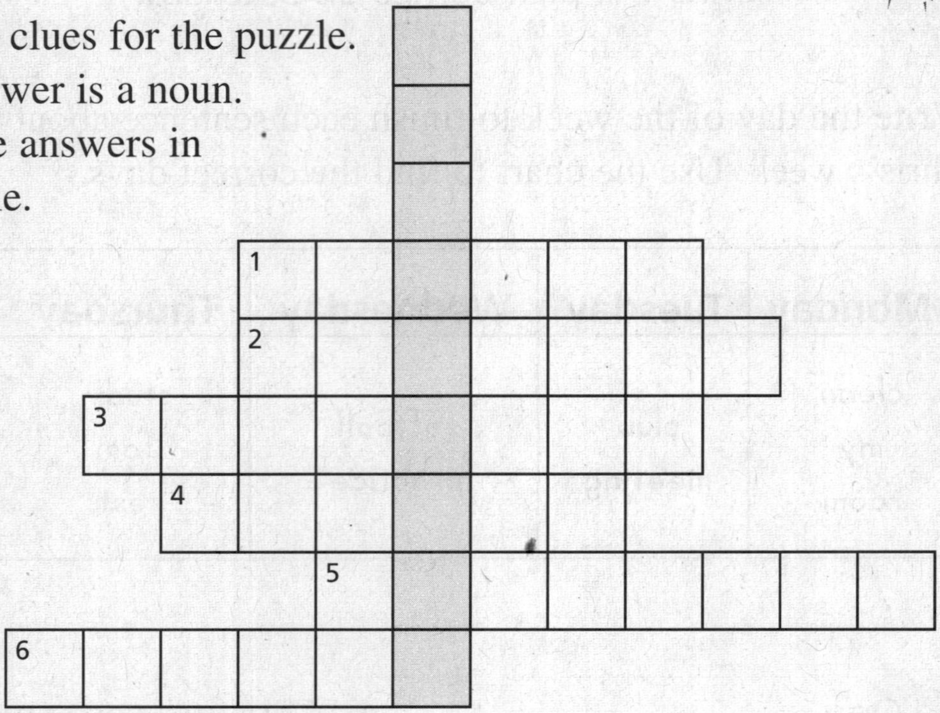

CLUES

1. the name of the day that comes after Sunday
2. the name of the day that comes after Monday
3. the name of the day that comes after Wednesday
4. the name of the day that comes before Saturday
5. the name of the day that comes after Friday
6. the name of the day that comes before Monday

Now find the hidden day of the week. Write three letters to finish the name of a day in the gray boxes.

Writing Application: Sentences

NARRATING

Write three sentences about things that you did last week. Use the names of three different days of the week.

Grade 2: Unit 9 More Capitalization and Punctuation (*Use with pupil book pages 297–298.*)
Skill: Students will write the names of the days of the week correctly.

Name ____________________

2 Holidays

People plant trees on **A**rbor **D**ay.
Valentine's **D**ay is February 14.

Write the sentences correctly.

1. I went sledding on new year's day.

2. February 2 is groundhog day.

3. We watched a parade on memorial day.

4. On mother's day we went on a picnic.

5. School starts right after labor day.

6. On thanksgiving day I always eat too much.

Name ______________________________

2 Holidays (continued from page 105)

Challenge

Choose four months. Look at a calendar. Write the name of a holiday that takes place in each month.

JANUARY

1	2	3	4	5	6	7
8	9	10	11	12	13	14
15	16	17	18	19	20	21
22	23	24	25	26	27	28
29	30	31				

FEBRUARY

			1	2	3	4
5	6	7	8	9	10	11
12	13	14	15	16	17	18
19	20	21	22	23	24	25
26	27	28				

MARCH

			1	2	3	4
5	6	7	8	9	10	11
12	13	14	15	16	17	18
19	20	21	22	23	24	25
26	27	28	29	30	31	

APRIL

						1
2	3	4	5	6	7	8
9	10	11	12	13	14	15
16	17	18	19	20	21	22
23	24	25	26	27	28	29
30						

MAY

	1	2	3	4	5	6
7	8	9	10	11	12	13
14	15	16	17	18	19	20
21	22	23	24	25	26	27
28	29	30	31			

JUNE

				1	2	3
4	5	6	7	8	9	10
11	12	13	14	15	16	17
18	19	20	21	22	23	24
25	26	27	28	29	30	

JULY

						1
2	3	4	5	6	7	8
9	10	11	12	13	14	15
16	17	18	19	20	21	22
23	24	25	26	27	28	29
30	31					

AUGUST

		1	2	3	4	5
6	7	8	9	10	11	12
13	14	15	16	17	18	19
20	21	22	23	24	25	26
27	28	29	30	31		

SEPTEMBER

					1	2
3	4	5	6	7	8	9
10	11	12	13	14	15	16
17	18	19	20	21	22	23
24	25	26	27	28	29	30

OCTOBER

1	2	3	4	5	6	7
8	9	10	11	12	13	14
15	16	17	18	19	20	21
22	23	24	25	26	27	28
29	30	31				

NOVEMBER

			1	2	3	4
5	6	7	8	9	10	11
12	13	14	15	16	17	18
19	20	21	22	23	24	25
26	27	28	29	30	31	

DECEMBER

						1
2	3	4	5	6	7	8
9	10	11	12	13	14	15
16	17	18	19	20	21	22
23	24	25	26	27	28	29
30	31					

Writing Application: A Description

DESCRIBING

Make up a new holiday. Tell the name of your holiday. Describe what people do on your holiday.

Grade 2: Unit 9 More Capitalization and Punctuation *(Use with pupil book pages 299–300.)*
Skill: Students will write the names of holidays and describe a new holiday.

Name ______________________

3 Months

January	**M**ay	**S**eptember
February	**J**une	**O**ctober
March	**J**uly	**N**ovember
April	**A**ugust	**D**ecember

A Write the sentences correctly. Begin the names of the months with capital letters.

1. Labor Day is in september.

____

2. Groundhog Day is in february.

____

B **3–6.** Proofread this part of a rhyme. Find four places to fix the names of months. Correct each mistake.

Example The first day of ~~january~~ January is New Year's Day.

Proofreading

Thirty days has september, April, june, and november.

All the rest have thirty-one, except february…

Name ________________________________

3 Months (continued from page 107)

Challenge

Write the names of the months to finish the puzzle.
Use the clues to help you.

1. Fall begins in this month.
2. We eat a turkey dinner in this month.
3. We start a new year in this month.
4. We see the trees change color in this month.
5. We fly kites in this windy month.

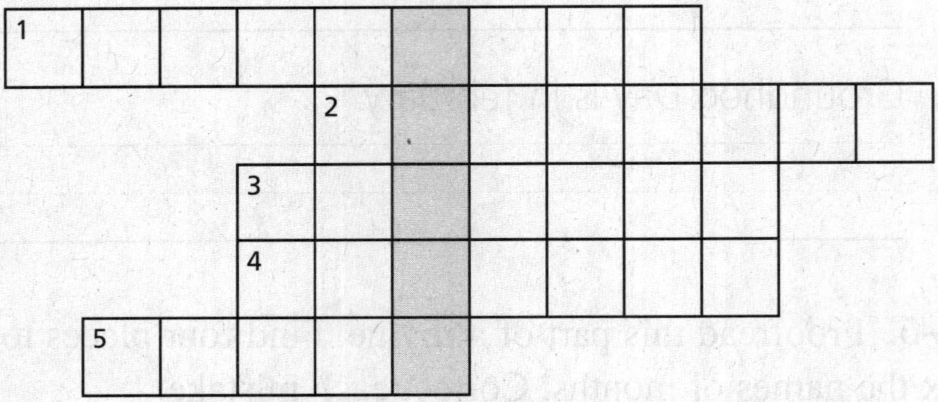

The letters in the gray boxes spell a word.

____

The word is ________________________________.

Writing Application: A Story

NARRATING

Write a story about something that happened in the month of your birthday. Be sure to write the name of the month correctly.

Grade 2: Unit 9 More Capitalization and Punctuation (*Use with pupil book pages 301–302.*)
Skill: Students will write the names of months and an original story.

Name ______________________________

4 Titles for People

A Read the poem. Find the three titles and names. Write them correctly on the lines below.

There was a man named mr Fray
Who swam the sea in a day, they say.
Along with dr Gray and mrs Clay,
He gathered starfish on the way.

1. ______________________ 2. ______________________

3. ______________________

B **4–6.** Proofread this part of a poster. Find three places to fix the titles of people. Correct each mistake.

Example Come see the amazing ~~ms~~ Ms. Maze!

Proofreading

Coming Soon! Amazing Circus!

See the great dr Juggle! Watch the brave ms. Swan fly through the air! See Mrs. Chiang's elephants! Hear Mr. Marvel's brass band! Look for miss Maypole the clown!

Name ______________________________

4 Titles for People (continued from page 109)

Challenge

Read the letter. The titles and the names of the people are not correct. Write them correctly.

Dear ms Blue,
I heard from miss gray that you are sick.
Go to see dr Hoad. He will make you better.
He helped my friend Mrs Ramirez.
Mr Smith and I will visit you tomorrow.
Your friend,
Lee

1. ____________________
2. ____________________
3. ____________________
4. ____________________
5. ____________________

Writing Application: Sentences

INFORMING

Write sentences about three grown-ups whom you like. Tell why you like them or what they do. Use each person's title.

Name ____________________

5 Writing Book Titles

Have you read Sylvester and the Magic Pebble?

Write these book titles correctly. Use capital letters correctly. Draw a line under each title.

1. arrow to the sun

2. a three hat day

3. a giraffe and a half

4. amelia bedelia and the baby

5. three by the sea

6. ramona the pest

Name ______________________

5 Writing Book Titles (continued from page 111)

Challenge

Make up a title for the book that each sentence tells about. Use capital letters correctly. Draw a line under each title.

This book is about an elephant who goes to the moon.

Example Elephant in Space Elephant in Space

1. This book is about a boy who won't wear shoes.

____

2. This book is about a lion who saves a lost prince.

____

3. This book is about a family who travels in a balloon.

____

4. This book is about a girl who builds a secret machine.

____

Writing Application: Sentences

DESCRIBING

Write some sentences about your favorite book. Use the title of the book in one of your sentences.

Grade 2: Unit 9 More Capitalization and Punctuation (*Use with pupil book pages 305–306.*)
Skill: Students will use titles correctly and will write original sentences.

Name ____________________

6 Ending Sentences

Printers make paper money. How do they make it?

A Write the sentences. Use the correct end mark for the telling sentence and the question.

1. Do printers use special paper

____

2. The printers use good ink

____

B **3–5.** Proofread this part of a survey. Find three places to add end marks. Correct each mistake.

Example Have you ever seen a five-dollar bill?

Proofreading

Money Survey

- Have you ever seen a ten-dollar bill

  No I haven't ever seen one

- Do you know how money is made?

  Not really, but I'd like to find out

Name ______________________

6 Ending Sentences (continued from page 113)

Challenge

Write the correct end mark for each telling sentence or question. Then write an answer to each question and a word to finish each telling sentence. Use the treasure map to help you.

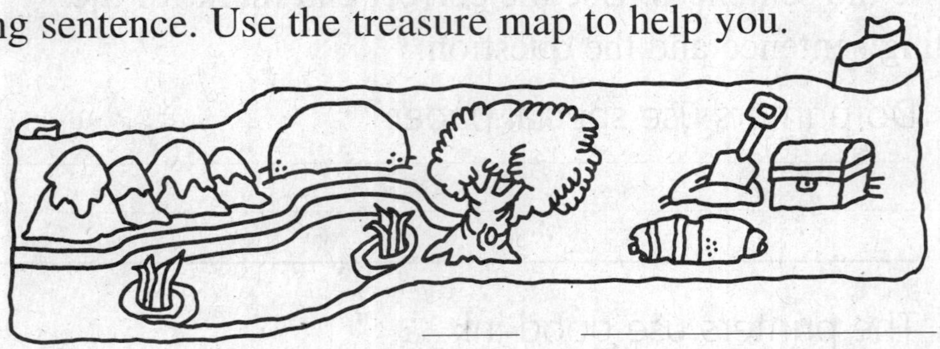

1. Do you go on the path ____ ______________
2. Does the path go by the lake ____ ______________
3. You turn ______________ at the big rock ____
4. You go to the old ______________ next ____
5. Then you walk ______________ steps ____

Writing Application: Sentences

CREATING

Suppose that you have a talking dollar bill. Write two questions that you would ask the dollar bill. Then write two telling sentences that the dollar bill might say.

Grade 2: Unit 9 More Capitalization and Punctuation (*Use with pupil book pages 307–308.*)
Skill: Students will write and punctuate original statements and questions.

Name ______________________________

Writing Correct Sentences

Wrong: Trees are important we need trees.

Right: Trees are important. We need trees.

Fixing Run-on Sentences 1-5. Find the run-on sentences. Turn them into shorter sentences. Write the new paragraph.

Trees do so many things for us. They give us shade they give us fruit to eat. Trees are homes for animals they are homes for birds. Trees also give us wood to build our homes the wood also keeps us warm. We should take care of our trees trees take care of us.

Name ______________________

Writing Correct Sentences

Wrong: Wanda swims every day she loves the water.

Right: Wanda swims every day. She loves the water.

Fixing Run-on Sentences Find the run-on sentences. Turn them into shorter sentences. Write the new sentences.

Wanda is always ready to jump in the pool. She likes to dive from the low board it is easier. Then she swims back and forth it is hard work. Once a week she takes lessons her teacher is very nice. Wanda will swim in a contest next week she will have a good time.

1. ______________________

2. ______________________

3. ______________________

4. ______________________

Grade 2: Unit 9 More Capitalization and Punctuation (*Use with pupil book pages 309–310.*)
Skill: Students will identify and correct run-on sentences.

Name ________________________

7 Commas in Dates

Louise was born April 6, 1981.

A Write each date correctly. Use a comma between the day and the year.

1. October 27 1983 ____________

2. June 13 1968 ____________

B Write the date in each sentence. Put a comma in the correct place.

3. Gram was born on August 2 1922.

____

4. Did she leave Greece on May 13 1946?

____

5. She arrived in the United States on June 4 1946.

____

Name ________________________________

7 Commas in Dates (continued from page 117)

Challenge

Help Josh finish his family tree. Put commas in the correct places in the sentences. Then write the correct dates in the family tree. Use the sentences to help you.

1. Mom was born on September 6 1954.
2. My sister Ruth was born on April 6 1984.
3. I was born on March 22 1981.
4. Dad was born on July 16 1951.

Poppa Woodly	Grandma Woodly	Grandpa Stewart	Grandma Stewart
June 2, 1929	March 6, 1933	May 30, 1928	July 9, 1926

Dad ________________________

Mom ________________________

Josh ________________________

Ruth ________________________

Writing Application: Sentences

NARRATING

What did you do yesterday? What are you going to do today? What will you do tomorrow? Write sentences to answer each question. Use a date in each sentence.

Grade 2: Unit 9 More Capitalization and Punctuation (*Use with pupil book pages 311–312.*)
Skill: Students will write dates correctly and write original sentences.

Name ______________________________

8 Commas with Names of Places

David has a pen pal who lives in Fairbanks**,** Alaska.

A Write the city and state named in each sentence. Put a comma in the correct place.

1. David got a card from Ira in Truckee California.

____

2. Ira is going to Reno Nevada.

____

3. Maura wrote from Atlanta Georgia.

____

B **4–6.** Proofread these ship's log entries. Find three places to add commas. Correct each mistake.

Example **September 12 — Long Beach, California**

Proofreading

Sept. 15 Oakland California

Oct. 2 Seattle Washington

Sept. 17 Honolulu Hawaii

Name ______________________

8 Commas with Names of Places (continued from page 119)

Challenge

Marcy lives in Springfield, Missouri. She and her mother took a trip. The map shows where they went. Finish Marcy's letter with the names of the cities and states that she visited.

Dear Jim,

Today we made our first stop in ______________________.

Tomorrow we will be in ______________________. On

Friday we will go on to ______________________. Then

we head for home.

Your friend,

Marcy

Writing Application: A Letter

INFORMING

Write a letter to a pen pal that you would like to have. Tell the pen pal the name of your city and state.

Grade 2: Unit 9 More Capitalization and Punctuation (*Use with pupil book pages 313–314.*)
Skill: Students will write the names of places correctly and will write a letter.

Name ______________________

9 Quotation Marks

José said, "I like to play the trumpet."

Write each sentence. Put quotation marks around exact words.

1. Leslie said, I like to play the drums.

2. Theo said, I like the drums also.

3. Ray asked, Is it hard to play piano?

4. Mr. Ramos replied, Not really, you just have to practice.

5. Jason said, I want to play the violin.

6. That's a good idea, said Rafael.

Name ______________________________

9 Quotation Marks (continued from page 121)

Challenge

Read the story. Then write each sentence that should have quotation marks.

> Once there was little mouse named Oliver. He was very quick. One day he met a bunny. Oliver asked, Where do you live? The bunny said, Over in the garden. Oliver said, It is good to be close to the garden. Yes it is, said the bunny. It is tasty, too! Then the bunny hopped right back home.

____

____

____

____

____

Writing Application: Quotation Marks

CREATING

Write a conversation between two friends. Have them talk about a movie they just saw.

Skill: Students will write quotation marks correctly and will write a conversation.

Name ______________________________

10 More About Quotation Marks

Dr. Laws said, "We will go camping tomorrow."

A Write the correct sentence in each pair.

1. Rami said, let's hike to the lake."

Rami said, "Let's hike to the lake."

____

2. Loren said, "I can hardly wait."

Loren said "I can hardly wait."

____

3. Steve said, I hear that there's beaver at the lake.

Steve said, "I hear that there's beaver at the lake."

____

B **4–6.** Proofread this part of a story. Find three places to fix quotations. Correct each mistake

Example Loren asked, "Where are the stars?"

Proofreading

Steve said, "There's no moon tonight.

Alan said, We'll see lots of stars."

Dr. Laws said, "look, you can see the Big Dipper."

Name ____________________

10 More About Quotation Marks (continued from page 123)

Challenge

Write a story about the picture. Use at least four sentences that have exact words that someone says.

Writing Application: More About Quotation Marks

NARRATING

Write a conversation between two friends who are sleeping outside at night.

Grade 2: Unit 9 More Capitalization and Punctuation (*Use with pupil book pages 317–318.*)

Skill: Students will write quotation marks correctly and write a conversation.

Name ______________________

Explaining with Examples

My opinion: I think blue is the nicest color of all.
Reason: The color blue makes me feel relaxed.
Example 1: I am relaxed at the beach and blue makes me think of the ocean.
Example 2: I feel relaxed at my grandma's house because she has blue curtains.

Write an opinion about a food you do or do not like. Then write one reason why you feel the way you do. Write two examples that explain the reason.

My Opinion: ______________________

Reason: ______________________

Example 1: ______________________

Example 2: ______________________

Name ______________________

Openings and Closings

Weak Opening	Strong Opening
I am writing about soccer.	I think soccer is a very cool sport.
Weak Closing	**Strong Closing**
I also like to play on a team.	Believe me, soccer is the greatest!

The opinion paragraph below needs an opening and a closing. Read the paragraph. Then write a strong opening and closing.

When you play basketball, no one stays still very long. Players have to dribble, pass, and run all the time. I also like basketball because I am good at it. I love the "swish" when I make a basket.

Strong Opening

____

____

Strong Closing

____

____

Grade 2: Unit 10 Opinion Essay (*Use with pupil book pages 351.*)
Skill: Students will write an opening and closing for an opinion essay.

Name ______________________

Writing with Voice

Weak Voice	Strong Voice
I go to Pinella Elementary. I like this school. The teachers are nice. My classmates are nice, too.	Pinella Elementary School is the best! The teachers help us with our work, and you can really tell they care.

The paragraph below is dull and boring. Rewrite it in your own voice. Use strong words that share an opinion.

People should treat animals kindly. Animals have feelings, too. People should take their dogs for a walk. People should brush their dogs and give them treats. Then the dogs will be happy. I feel strongly about this.

Name ______________________________

Revising an Opinion Essay

Have I	**yes**
• stated my opinion clearly and in an interesting way?	☐
• written good reasons and examples?	☐
• used words that show my feelings?	☐
• told my opinion again at the end, using different words?	☐

Revise this paragraph to make it better. Check off each box to be sure. You can write your changes in the spaces above each line, on the sides, and below the paragraph.

Pizza is party food because everyone likes it. I don't know anyone who doesn't like pizza. You can add different things. Everyone can have what they like. Also, pizza doesn't cost a lot. One large pie feeds four people for only a few dollars each. That's why pizza is good.

Grade 2: Unit 10 Opinion Essay (*Use with pupil book page 353.*)
Skill: Students will revise an opinion essay, using a checklist as a guide.

Name ______________________________

Revising Strategies: Word Choice

Three boys rode Harvest Fair
~~They~~ ^ ~~went~~ ^ to the ^ ~~event.~~

Revise each sentence. Add exact nouns, adjectives, and verbs to make the sentences interesting.

1. I think she works hard.

____

2. They went to a city.

____

3. He liked the book.

____

4. I liked the food we ate.

____